The Gr
LOVE SONGS
Of The 70s

CW00495000

Wise Publications
part of **The Music Sales Group**
London/New York/Paris/Sydney/Copenhagen/Berlin/Madrid/Tokyo

Published by

Wise Publications
14-15 Berners Street, London WIT 3LJ, UK.

Exclusive Distributors:

Music Sales Limited
Distribution Centre, Newmarket Road,
Bury St Edmunds, Suffolk IP33 3YB, UK.

Music Sales Pty Limited
120 Rothschild Avenue, Rosebery,
NSW 2018, Australia.

Order No. AM986799
ISBN 1-84609-708-8
This book © Copyright 2006 Wise Publications,
a division of Music Sales Limited.

Front cover photo courtesy of Jupiter Images.
Back cover photos; Leo Sayer. - Pieter Mazel/LFI,
Olivia Newton-John, Rod Stewart & Gladys Knight/LFI,
David Soul - Brad Elterman/LFI.

Printed in the EU.

www.musicsales.com

Your Guarantee of Quality

As publishers, we strive to produce every book
to the highest commercial standards.

The book has been carefully designed
to minimise awkward page turns and to
make playing from it a real pleasure.

Particular care has been given to specifying
acid-free, neutral-sized paper made from pulps
which have not been elemental chlorine bleached.

This pulp is from farmed sustainable forests and
was produced with special regard for the environment.

Throughout, the printing and binding have been
planned to ensure a sturdy, attractive publication
which should give years of enjoyment.

If your copy fails to meet our high standards,
please inform us and we will gladly replace it.

Ain't No Sunshine

Words & Music by Bill Withers

§ Am   Em7   Am   Em7

gone,   won der if___ she's_ gone to stay.)
gone,   on - ly dark - ness__ ev - 'ry day.)

Am   Em

Ain't no sun - shine when she's gone,_____ and this house just ain't no

Dm7   Am   Em7   *To Coda* ⊕

home an - y - time___ she goes a - way.

Am

N.C.

And I know, I know, I know,_ I know, I know, I know, I know,_ I know,_ I know I

5

Always On My Mind

Words & Music by Mark James, Wayne Thompson & Johnny Christopher

9

Baby, I Love Your Way

Words & Music by Peter Frampton

1. Sha - dows grow so long_ be - fore my eyes and they're
(Verses 2 & 3 see block lyrics)

13

14

Verse 2:
Moon appears to shine and light the sky
With the help of some fire-fly
I wonder how they have the power to shine
I can't see them under the pine
But don't hesitate 'cos your love won't wait.

Ooh, baby I love your way *etc.*

Verse 3:
I can see the sunset in your eyes
Brown and grey and blue besides
Clouds are stalking islands in the sun
I wish I could buy one out of season
But don't hesitate 'cos your love won't wait.

Ooh, baby I love your way *etc.*

Can't Give You Anything (But My Love)

Words & Music by Hugo Peretti, Luigi Creatore & George David Weiss

17

but my love. I

can't give you a - ny - thing but my love,

but my love.

2. I can-not

D.%. and fade

18

Can't Smile Without You

Words & Music by Chris Arnold, David Martin & Geoff Morrow

you're   glad,   if   you___   on - ly   knew   what   I'm___   go - ing   through;

I   just   can't   smile___   with - out   you.

You   came   a - long___   just   like   a   song___   and   bright - ened   my   day.___

Who'd - a   be - lieved   that   you   were   part   of   a   dream.___   Now   it   all   seems

20

you____ on - ly knew what I'm____ go - ing through; I just can't

smile.____ Now, some peo - ple say____ hap - pi - ness takes____ so____ ve - ry long to find.___

____ Well, I'm find - ing it hard____ leav - ing your love be - hind

me. And you see, I can't smile with - out you,

22

I can't smile with-out you, I can't laugh and I can't sing, I'm finding it hard to do a-ny-thing. You see, I feel glad when you. you're glad, I feel sad when you're sad, if you on-ly knew what

Instrumental till fade

I'm go-ing through; I just can't smile with-out

Repeat and fade

23

Don't Give Up On Us

Words & Music by Tony Macaulay

D.S. al Coda

3. Don't give

Coda

through._____

It's writ-ten in the moon-light   and paint-ed on the

27

stars. We can't change___ ours. Don't give

up on us ba - by, we're still___ worth___ one more

try. I know we've put a last one___ by,___

just for a rain - y eve - ning when may - be stars are

28

The First Time Ever I Saw Your Face

Words & Music by Ewan MacColl

The first time ever I saw your face,

(Verses 2 & 3 see block lyrics)

I thought the sun

Verse 2

The first time ever I kissed your mouth
I felt the earth move in my hand,
Like the trembling heart of a captive bird
That was there at my command, my love,
That was there at my command.

Verse 3

The first time ever I lay with you
And felt your heart so close to mine,
And I knew our joy would fill the earth
And last till the end of time, my love.
The first time ever I saw your face,
Your face, your face, your face.

Hopelessly Devoted To You

Words & Music by John Farrar

eyes   are not the first   to_____ cry._____   I'm

not   the first   to   know   there's just   no   get - ting   ov   -   -   er

you._____   2. I

know   I'm just   a   fool   who's_____   will - ing_____   to
head   is   say - ing "Fool,   for - get   him."_____   My

38

How Deep Is Your Love

Words & Music by Barry Gibb, Maurice Gibb & Robin Gibb

feel you in my arms a - gain._____ And you come_____ to me_____ on a sum -
sav - iour_____ when I fall._____ And you may_____ not think_____ I____ care____

- mer breeze;_____ keep me warm_____ in your love,_____ then you soft -
____ for you_____ when you know_____ down in - side_____ that I real -

(how deep is your love?)

- ly leave.____ And it's me you need____ to show:_____ How deep
- ly do.____ And it's me you need____ to show:_____ How deep

___ is your love?_____ How deep_____ is your_____ love?

40

41

I Don't Know How To Love Him

Words by Tim Rice
Music by Andrew Lloyd Webber

I Don't Want To Talk About It

Words & Music by Danny Whitten

Jealous Guy

Words & Music by John Lennon

Love And Affection

Words & Music by Joan Armatrading

why can't_ I_____ feel_____ love?_____ I can real - ly love,__ real - ly love,__ real - ly love,__ real - ly love,__ real - ly love.__ Love, love, love, love,_ love. Love, love, love. Now I got all_____

Make love,__ oh,_____
(Lov - er ooh hoo.)

Lovin' You

Words & Music by
Minnie Riperton & Richard Rudolph

Midnight Train To Georgia

Words & Music by Jim Weatherly

leav - in'____ (leav-in') on____ that mid-night train____to Geor - gia.(Leavin' on that mid-night train.___)

Yes, said he's go-in' back (go-in' back____ to find) to a sim-pler

place and time. Oh yes he is. And I'll____ be with him (I know you will____
(When-ev-er he takes that ride____ guess who's gonna be right by____ his side.___)

____) on____ that mid-night train to Geor - gia. Hey._____
(Leav-in on the mid-night train____ to Geor-gia, woo woo!)

68

Verse 2:

He kept dreamin' that someday he'd be the star
(A superstar, but he didn't get far)
But he sure found out the hard way
That dreams don't always come true
So he turned all his hopes
And he even sold his old car
Bought a one-way ticket back to the life he once knew.

He's leavin' *etc.*

My Love

Words & Music by
Paul McCartney & Linda McCartney

She

Words by Herbert Kretzmer
Music by Charles Aznavour

sings, ____ may be the chill that au - tumn brings, ____ may be a hun - dred diff - 'rent

things _____ with - in the mea - sure of a day.

2. She ____ may be the beau - ty or the beast, ____ may be the fa - mine or the
(Verse 3 instr., Verse 4 see block lyric)

feast,___ may turn each day in-to a hea - ven or___ hell.

She___ may be the mir - ror of my dreams___ a smile re - flect - ed in a

To Coda ⊕

stream,___ she may not be what she may seem, in - side her

D.S. al Coda

⊕ *Coda*

She__ may be the love that can-not hope to last,__ may come to me from sha-dows of the past_____ that I'll re-mem - ber till the day I die.

She, she,_____ she.

Verse 4
She may be the reason I survive
The why and wherefore I'm alive
The one I'll care for through the rough and ready years.
Me, I'll take her laughter and her tears
And make them all my souvenirs
For where she goes I've got to be.
The meaning of my life is she, she, she.

77

So You Win Again

Words & Music by Russ Ballard

Do do do do,   do do do do,   do do do do.

1. Just to ad-mit   one mis-take__   it can be hard to take.__

(Verse 2 see block lyric)

took my love and run,__ but love had just be - gun.__ I can't re - fuse her__ and

now I know__ that I'm the fool__ who won your love__ to

lose it all,__ when you've come back you win a - gain.__

Verse 2
And I'm not proud to say I let love slip away
Now I'm the one who's crying
I'm a fool, there's no denying
When will my heartache end?
Will my whole life depend on fading memories?
You took the game this time with ease.

So you win again *etc.*

If You Leave Me Now

Words & Music by Peter Cetera

Original key: B major

things we said__ to - day._____ If you

leave me now__ you'll take a - way the big - gest part__ of me,__

ooh_____ no,____ ba - by, please_____ don't go.____

Ooh,_____ girl, _____ just _____ got to have_ you by _____ my _____ side._____

Ooh,____

no, baby, please don't go.

Ooh, ma - ma, I've just got to have your lov - ing, yeah.

Repeat and fade

92

Sometimes When We Touch

Words by Dan Hill
Music by Barry Mann

Em7　　　D/F#　　　A

see the real＿＿＿ you.＿
trapped with-in＿＿ my youth.＿
pas-sion flares＿ a - gain.＿

And

D　　　　G　　　A　　　F#m

some-times when we touch,＿ the hon-es-ty's＿ too＿ much.＿

And I

Bm　　　　E　　　　A　　　G

have to close＿ my eyes＿ and＿＿＿ hide.＿

F#m　　Em　　D　　　　G

I wan-na hold you till＿ I die,＿

till we

mp - mf - f

95

A
F♯m
both break down and cry. I wan-na
Em7
G/A
3 fr.
To Coda
hold you till the fear in me sub-
1. D
D7
G/D
sides.
Gm/D
Ro-
2. D
A/D
G/D
D
sides. At
cresc.

Sorry Seems To Be
The Hardest Word

Words & Music by Elton John & Bernie Taupin

What have I got-ta do to make you love___ ___ me?___ What have I got-ta do___ to make_ you care?___

D.S. al Coda

Coda

What do I do   to make you love___   me?

What have I got - ta   do___   to___   be   heard?___

102

What do I do when light-ning strikes me?

What have I got-ta do?___ What have I got-ta do?_____ And

sor-ry seems to be_____ the hard-est word.

rit.

103

Talking In Your Sleep

Words & Music by Roger Cook & Bobby Wood

you used to _____ love me

Cm7   F   F7   F aug5   F

talk - in' in ___ your ___ sleep   with lov - in'   on ___

Bbm7   Eb7

1

your ___ mind _____

Ab   Eb7/Ab

2

your ___ mind ___   You've been talk - in' in ___ your ___ sleep

Ab   Eb7/Ab   Ab

106

We've Only Just Begun

Words by Paul Williams
Music by Roger Nichols

1. We've on - ly just be - gun to live, white lace and
(2, 3 & 4° see block lyric)

prom - i - ses, a kiss for luck and we're on our way.

2°
Before the rising sun we fly
So many roads to choose
We start out walking and learn to run.

3°
And when the evening comes we smile
So much of life ahead
We'll find a place where there's room to grow

4°
And when the evening comes we smile
So much of life ahead
We'll find a place where there's room to grow

Where Do I Begin
(Theme from 'Love Story')

Words by Carl Sigman
Music by Francis Lai

Where do I be - gin _____ to tell the sto - ry of how
With her first hel - lo _____ she gave a mean - ing to this

great a love can be, _____ the sweet love sto - ry that is
emp - ty world of mine. _____ There'd nev - er be an - oth - er

old - er than the sea, the sim - ple truth a - bout the
love, an - oth - er time; she came in - to my life and

110

111

When I Need You

Words & Music by Albert Hammond & Carole Bayer Sager

When I need you, I just close my eyes and I'm with you and

all that I so want to give you, it's on-ly a heart-beat a - way.___ When I

need love, I hold out my hands and I touch love, I nev - er knew there was so

much love, keep-ing me warm night and day.___

Miles and miles of emp-ty space in be - tween us, a
It's not ea - sy when the road is your dri - ver,

give you ba - by, it's on - ly a heart - beat a - way.

do like I do.

When I

need love, I hold out my hands and I touch love, _____ and I

Repeat ad lib. to fade

118

Your Song

Words & Music by Elton John & Bernie Taupin

Don't have much mo - ney,_ but,_ boy, if_ I did,_
I know it's not much,_ but_ it's the best_ I_ can do._

I'd buy_ big house where_ we both_ could
My gift_ is my song, yeah;_

live. this one's_ for you._

And you_ can tell ev - 'ry - bo - dy

Coda

words   how won - der - ful life is while

you're in the world.

I hope you don't mind, I hope you don't mind that I put down in

words   how won - der - ful life is while

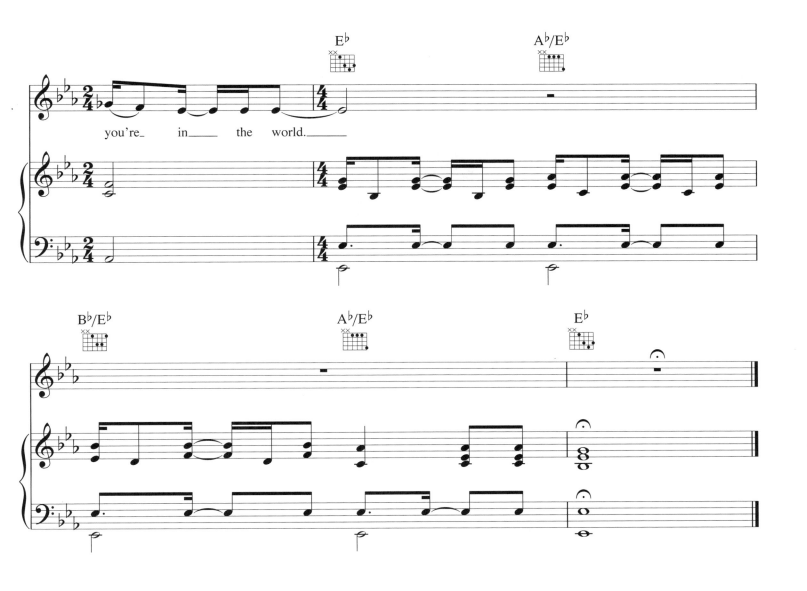

you're_ in___ the world.___

Verse 3:
I sat on the roof and kicked off the moss.
Well, a few of the verses, well, they've got me quite cross,
But the sun's been quite kind while I wrote this song;
It's for the people like you that keep it turned on.

Verse 4:
So excuse me forgetting, but these things I do;
You see I've forgotten if they're green or they're blue.
Anyway, the thing is, what I really mean;
Yours are the sweetest eyes I've ever seen.

And you can tell everybody *etc.*

Wonderful Tonight

Words & Music by Eric Clapton

1. It's late in the eve - ning,
2. We go to a par - ty,
3. It's time to go home __ now,

she's won-d'ring what clothes __ to wear. __
and ev - 'ry-one turns __ to see __
and I've got an ach - ing head. __

She puts on her make-
this beau - ti - ful la -
So I give her the car __

D.𝄋.al Coda

⊕Coda

Oh, my dar-ling, you are won-der - ful _____ to - night." _

rit.

1 2 3 4 5 6 7 8 9